Grateful and Generous Hearts

A Pilgrim's Stewardship Adventure

by

The Rev. Dr. John H. Westerhoff

"Moses said to all the congregation ... the Lord
has commanded: Take from among you an
offering to the Lord; let whoever is of a grateful
and generous heart bring the Lord's offering ..."

Exodus 35:4-5

A Note from the Author

Shortly after leaving the faculty of the Duke University Divinity School to return to my first love, the parish, I was encouraged to become the founding director of an Institute for Pastoral Studies whose purpose would be to serve the needs of the Episcopal Church in the Diocese of Atlanta and throughout the country. Among our various projects was to be the publication of educational resources on a variety of subjects. I decided on a series of short monographs, the first being *A People Called Episcopalians*, to be used in inquirer classes and other programs for new and longtime Episcopalians. The second was *Holy Baptism: A Guide for Parents and Godparents*. Both have been popular, and recently I began to receive requests for a resource on stewardship for the use of vestries, stewardship committees, new members, stewardship programs and study groups. And so I wrote *Grateful and Generous Hearts*, with the hope that it will prove as useful as the others.

In the years ahead our publishing program will continue with: *To Love and to Cherish, Till Death Do Us Part: Preparing for the Celebration and Blessing of a Marriage, Growing in Our Relationship with God: Spiritual Healing, Reconciliation, and Spiritual Friendship*, and *The Making of Christians: A New Look at Formation, Education and Instruction*.

I would like to express my gratitude to Marcia Murphy for design and production and to Sara Wood for her editorial assistance.

A Reader's Guide

The primary purpose of this short book is not to advocate a particular point of view or engage in a debate, although it will present a personal set of convictions and perhaps be controversial. Its primary purpose is to educate, that is, to offer a resource to stimulate reflection on what may be the church's most important spiritual concern: stewardship. It is the culmination of a personal fifty years of struggle. My hope is that even those who find it unreasonable will take it seriously and not discard it without serious consideration.

Therefore, after you have read through this manuscript, I encourage you to go back and read it again and mark those places where you agree and disagree, those statements which left you with questions to consider, and those issues you would like to discuss.

Next, review your positive and negative reactions. What insights or learnings can you gain from them? Rather than arguing with my thoughts, what can you learn about your life as a believer in Jesus Christ and a member of his church, especially from those statements which made you uncomfortable or upset?

Having named your insights and learnings, what are their implications for your life and the life of your congregation?

Now join or form a group of persons who have also reflected on this manuscript and share your reactions, insights, and their implications. Also share and discuss the concerns and questions which surfaced during your reading of this tract on stewardship.

Perhaps there are statements you would like to share with others in some manner. Remember, my aim is to provide a resource for you to grow personally and to use in the development of a program of steward-ship in your congregation.

And thank you now for giving this very personal polemic on stewardship as a spiritual issue a serious reading.

ⓞpening ℛeflections

At our baptism each of us was made a Christian. However, insofar as Christianity is a way of life, each of us is called upon to live in commu-nity and enter upon a pilgrimage to become Christian, that is, to live into our baptism and become the person our baptism proclaims we are. This pilgrimage is an adventure and a difficult challenge, particularly in terms of becoming a faithful steward.

One of the major reasons that it is difficult for us either to understand or become faithful stewards is that we live in a functional era, a time in which our being is defined by our doing. In other words, we are what we do.

As followers of Jesus, however, we cannot separate who we are from how we behave. But neither can we begin with our behavior. We must begin always with whom God has made us, that is, with our being, who by God's grace we really are.

Our identity is to be founded upon the fact that we have been incorporated into the body of Christ to the end that we might have Christlike characteristics, that is, be disposed to behave in Christlike ways. (I refer you to *Calling: A Song for the Baptized*, by Caroline Westerhoff, Cowley Publications.)

One of the difficulties in understanding stewardship in our functional era is that most people's understanding focuses on action, trying to convince people to give of their time, talents, and treasures to the laudatory programs and faithful works of the church. Nevertheless, this essay is not concerned with raising money or gaining more volunteers for the church. Therefore, I invite you to put aside all your present understandings and all you have been taught about stewardship and consider an alternative.

What follows is about God's invitation to enter upon a pilgrimage of living into your baptism, of acquiring a more grateful and generous heart, a heart like Jesus'.

Much Obliged, Dear Lord

Fulton Oursler, author of *The Greatest Story Ever Told*,[1] tells the story of Anna, the old black woman who raised him as a child. One day, he writes, he was sitting in the kitchen and heard her say, "Much obliged, dear Lord, for my vittles."

"What's a vittle?" he asked.

"It's whatever I've got to eat and drink," she responded.

"But you'd get your vittles whether you thanked God or not!" he continued.

"Sure," she said, "but it makes everything taste better to be thankful. You know, it's a game an old preacher taught me to play. It's about looking for things to be thankful for. Like one day I was walking to the store to buy a loaf of bread. I look in all the windows. There are so many pretty clothes."

"But Anna, you can't afford to buy any of them!" he interjected.

"Oh, I know, but I can play dolls with them. I can imagine your mom and sister all dressed up in them and I'm thankful. Much obliged, dear Lord, for playing in an old lady's mind."

"Then," she continued, "one day, I got caught in the rain. I had heard about people taking showers and I've seen the one you use, and I thought, now I have one too. You know, God is just giving away heaven every day. Much obliged, dear Lord."

4

Oursler ends his story with these words: "The soul of long-dead Anna was a big soul, big enough to see God everywhere, and she taught me a great deal about life; for I will never forget when word came to me from the dingy street where she lived that Anna was dying. I remember driving in a cab and standing by her bedside; she was deep in pain and her old hands were knotted together in a desperate clutch. Poor old woman, what had she to be thankful for now?"

"She opened her eyes and looked at me. 'Much obliged, dear Lord, for such fine friends.' She never spoke again except in my heart, but she speaks to me every day there, and I'm much obliged, dear Lord, for that."

This is much more than a moving Pollyanna story. Anna was not simply an optimistic personality, one who, no matter what, could look on the bright side of things. She was, in Oursler's words, "a big soul, big enough to see God everywhere." She was in her heart a grateful person, one who had a deep sense that all of life is a gift. Taking nothing for granted, demanding nothing as her due, she recognized that we come into this world with nothing, we go out with nothing, and in between we are given all we have.

To be thankful is not to deny that life can be difficult and painful. It does not compel us to pretend that things are better than they are or to ignore the suffering and pain in our lives or in the lives of others. But being thankful does require us to acknowledge our creaturehood, our dependence, and our lack of self-sufficiency. And it does require us to express through grateful and generous hearts our thankfulness. "Much obliged, dear Lord, for all you have given us."

Perception Is Everything

How we understand and live our lives is a result of how we perceive life and our lives. Christianity is a way of life dependent upon our perceptions, which is to say our faith. We all live by some faith. And that faith determines how we live.

Recall the parable of the talents (Matthew 25:14–30). It is a story that is related to stewardship, but not in the way we might think. In this story, like many others, there are two throwaway characters whose purpose is to draw attention to a third character. In this case, there is the master, who is God. God entrusts his three servants with his money. God returns and asks them to account for their stewardship. The third one explains, "I perceived you to be a harsh, demanding, critical parent, and so I saved what you gave me and here it is." And God responds, "You say I am a harsh, demanding, critical parent? Well then, let's take what you have saved and give it to the others, and then cast you out where there is gnashing of teeth."

Here is a parable intended to teach us that the God we perceive is the only God we can experience, even if the God of our experience is not God at all. Further, this faith or perception of God will influence our understanding of stewardship. Stewardship, therefore, is first of all about how we perceive life and our lives—about faith.

Stewardship is one dimension of the Christian life of faith. It is not a program, not an every-member canvass, not a fund-raising campaign, not an occasion for people to vote whether they like or do not like how the church spends their money or treats them.

Stewardship is what we do after we say **Credo**, we believe, that is, after we give our love, loyalty, trust and obedience to God, the God of our faith.

Christian faith, I acknowledge, makes little sense in the modern world. It is a perception of life in which everything we have and are is gift. It perceives that we are called to be servants of the master, ministers of the magister, stewards of God.

A Confession

My theology of stewardship has always been orthodox. My problem, however, was that what I believed in my head I did not believe in my heart. To be personal and I hope not self-serving, for many years I had difficulty living faithfully in terms of my stewardship of money. I rationalized. I worked long and hard for everything I earned, for less than I reasoned I was worth and my family deserved. I made my contribution to the church through my labor, my time and my talents. And while I made a pledge each year, it was very little. As you may guess, I never preached on stewardship. I told my parishioners that the financial aspect of the church's life was their responsibility. Over the years my guilt increased, for I knew my stewardship was poor and my life of faith flawed.

Then a number of years ago, Caroline, with whom I had worked for many years, and I talked about the possibility of marriage. Early on she made it quite clear that if we did marry we were going to pledge a minimum of ten percent of all our earnings to the church and it would be the first check written each month. That was the beginning of my conversion.

Amidst these conversations on stewardship two memories surfaced. The first was working with Caroline in New York sometime earlier. We had finished a long day and were going out for supper. Walking up Fifth Avenue, we looked down and there was a large bill in a doorway of a closed business. She picked it up, looked around, and saw that no one around us seemed to have lost it. I'm embarrassed to say my first thought was that it would take care of supper. We walked a few feet. In front of us was a group of street musicians. Caroline dropped the bill into their offering basket, saying, "It came from the street—it needs to go back to the street."

The second was a conversation with Peter Lee, the present bishop of Virginia, who was at one time my rector, colleague, and friend at the Chapel of the Cross in Chapel Hill, North Carolina. One day he told me of his father during an economic recession. While he was in college, he sent a letter to Peter saying that he was experiencing some financial difficulties. He explained that he would not consider cutting or even reducing his pledge, his promise to the church. That would be paid first, no matter what, so Peter had better find a job and apply for a scholarship because otherwise he would need to drop out of school.

Today, Caroline and I do tithe. I feel good about that, and now I have no trouble talking about money and stewardship. Our habit is to pay by check, the first written each month. But Caroline, who sits in a pew most weeks, insists on making an additional weekly contribution because she believes that this symbolic action is an important part of the liturgy. She also lives by an important principle, namely that if there is only one bill in her wallet, that is what she will offer. She came home a few months ago and with a glint in her eyes told me of her morning's struggle of conscience when she looked in her wallet and discovered that all she had was a very large bill. Then she looked at me and said, "What do you think I did?" "That's easy," I responded. "You gave it!" "Right," she said. "I'm glad you did," I commented with a chuckle, "but next time why not check your wallet before you come to church." I knew she wouldn't.

The Economics of God

One of our problems in the church is that we rarely discuss the relationship of theology and economics, the economics of God. Rarely do future clergy study economics in seminary, or future business executives study theology in business school. For too long we have appeared content to maintain a heretical dualism between a material and spiritual world. Regretfully, it is a position still present in the church's canons, which speak of the vestry being responsible for the temporal affairs of the church and the rector the spiritual.

Nevertheless, for Christians there can be only one reality and it is spiritual, a reality that has two dimensions, one material and the other nonmaterial. For this reason, when we discuss the spiritual

life in the church we need to include the material, that is, money.
As we correct this misunderstanding and consider the spiritual life and
the economics of God we become aware that we have typically misinterpreted the biblical tithe. For example, the tithe of ten percent of all
one's holdings was to be an expected beginning point, not a goal to work
toward. In fact, there is some evidence that there might have been two
tithes, one paid to the temple and priests and the other to the poor and
the needy. And when the people came to worship they were to bring
both tithes and offerings. The offerings were a tithe of their time and
talents to the service of God and the needy.

More importantly, the tithe was not a means to raise money or pay for
services. The intent of these tithes and offerings was spiritual and
symbolic. Just as there was once a custom that the faithful were to fast,
not eat or drink, before communion to remind themselves of the food
they need most for life, our tithes and offerings were to remind us what
we need most for life—not material things or the things money can buy,
but an ever deepening and loving relationship with God.

This idea of the economics of God may make little sense in our
materialistic culture, but I can testify that once I understood and
accepted it, my question was no longer "What do I need to give?" but
"What do I have a right to keep?" And the answer is "Not much." I am
still not as grateful or generous as I should be, and I have a long way to
go before I do as I know I need to do. But I am quite convinced that
there is a direct correlation between my relationship with God and my
giving of myself and my economic resources to the service of God.

I therefore need and expect the church to remind me, encourage me,
and support me in growing into an ever deepening and loving relationship with God so that I might become a more faithful steward. This
relationship with God is our only end, and everything else is to be

understood as a means to that end. I know that now and have never been happier in my life.

Stewardship is the way to spiritual health and maturity, but for stewardship to have a chance we must begin with a serious spiritual question: What do we owe to God for the free gift of life and its accompanying benefits? The answer, of course, is everything. And that means we need to reject the all-too-common conviction that what we have personally earned, deserved, acquired, or won is ours to possess and do with as we see fit.

Our challenge is to make this text from Frank von Christierson's hymn our own: "As those of old their first fruits brought of vineyard, flock, and field to God, the giver of all good, the source of bounteous yield; so we today our first fruits bring, the wealth of this good land, of farm and market, shop and home, of mind and heart and hand" (705, Hymnal 1982).

As a statement of faith this hymn makes clear that everything we have and are belongs to God. That "All things come from you, O Lord, and of your own have we given you" is a conviction, however, is not self-evident and impossible to prove by logic. It is a matter of faith.

At the heart of Anglican theology is the incarnation, the spirit dwelling in matter, the dwelling of God within creation. God's spirit is within us, among us, beyond us, and beneath us. The separateness we have created between religion and economics is the result of a false consciousness. As Anglicans whose understanding of the spiritual life is materialistic, we need to ponder and practice the economic implications of "God with us."

11

It Just Isn't Easy to Accept or Comprehend

Recall the story Jesus told about paying taxes (Matthew 22:15–22). The religious folk were always trying to trap Jesus. "Teacher, we know that you are right in what you say and that you teach the way of God in accordance with truth," they say to him one day. (Now there is a set-up!) "Is it then lawful for us to pay taxes to the emperor or not?" Not easily tricked, Jesus takes the coin and asks whose head and whose title it bears. They answer, "The emperor's." "Right, then give the emperor the things that are his and give to God that which is God's." Caught! They knew they bore on their souls the image of God. Their very lives belonged to God. For it is God who made us and not we ourselves. We may owe a few coins to the emperor for taxes, but we owe everything—all our time, our talents, and our treasures—to God.

Still, we typically talk of our money, our abilities, our home, our degree, our possessions, our life, our job, our church, our accomplishments. Have you ever noticed that the possessive dominates how we talk? We say I have a car, a home, a job, a degree, a mate and so forth.

One day a woman came to me in tears. She explained, "I do not have any friends." I responded, "Please listen carefully. I do not want to make you feel bad and I do hear your pain. But I'm not sad that you have no friends. You see, no one can *have* friends, that is, possess another. The issue for all of us is not in having a friend but being a friend."

And yet, the dominant metaphor of our culture is owning. We own a point of view. We say, "I'll buy that." Our worth is often judged by how much we contribute and participate, not who we are. Yet for Jesus our worth is our being, our character, the manner in which we are disposed to behave and the motives behind our behavior. Recall the woman with the small coin who was praised because of her gift (Luke 21:1–4). In gratitude to God for her blessings she offered her tithe joyfully. And while it amounted to almost nothing, as compared to the scant amount given grudgingly by the rich man, she was the one Jesus called faithful.

Consider how often we use the language of reward and punishment. We talk of people getting what they deserve. We believe that if we work hard and do well we deserve it. And sometimes we accuse the homeless and the poor of being unwilling to work and therefore of not deserving.

Such thoughts are not new, which explains why Jesus told the story of the vineyard (Matthew 20:1–16). Let me retell it in a modern version. A group of young white males are hired early in the day at a high rate of pay. At noon the owner notices some Afro-Americans and Hispanics, who often have difficulty finding good jobs at the gate, and he hires them. Later he notices a group of mothers with their children who need work. He has one woman open a nursery to care for the children and hires the others. Then just before the end of the workday he notices some older people who have been forced to retire and he hires them. Shortly thereafter he closes up for the day and gives all the workers the same daily pay. The young white males are very unhappy and believe that they have been treated unfairly. The owner simply asks, "Why are you so upset about my generosity?" You see, in the economics of God we are not given what we deserve (I might add, thank God), we are given what we need. And that, incidentally, is how we also are to live, seeing that all people receive what they need rather than what they deserve.

Acquiring the Faith of a Good Steward

But how does one come to have such a faithful way to perceive the economics of God?

"The world is charged with the grandeur of God," begins a poem written over a hundred years ago. Its author was Gerard Manley Hopkins, a Jesuit priest. Hopkins used his dual gifts of deep faith and poetic expression to inspire and enliven the faith of others.

Robert Bridges, with whom Hopkins shared his poems, was one of those touched by Hopkins' deep and abiding faith. Bridges, haunted by his own lack of faith, wrote to Hopkins asking him to explain how he, Bridges, might share in that faith. From such a gifted visionary, theologian and linguist we might have expected a lengthy, elaborate response. Instead Hopkins wrote back, "Give alms."

The advice to give alms tells us first that faith is a gift given to those who act in faith. Rather than sitting around wishing we had faith, we need to step out boldly and act in faith. Never forget that we are more apt to act our way into a new way of thinking than think our way into a new way of acting.

Second, the advice to give alms, to give freely and generously of ourselves and our possessions in love, is to make a step in the direction of growing into an ever deepening and loving relationship with God. In sharing generously with others what we have been given by God, we grow in the life of faith.

And, third, in giving alms we learn that life with God is an exchange of gifts. The world, which is charged with the grandeur of God, is God's benevolent gift to each of us. And we appropriately express our gratitude for all that God has given to us by giving alms for the benefit of that very world.

In the story of Lazarus and the rich man (Luke 16:19–31), Jesus introduces us to one who did not give alms. He seemed not to give much of anything. He was blessed with an abundance of the world's goods, but he had no awareness that it was charged with the grandeur of God. He was oblivious to the needs of the world. As far as we know, it never occurred to him that Lazarus might want the food the dogs were getting. As long as the rich man's own needs were consistently and fully met, he was content. He may have had some sense of gratitude, but not enough to be truly generous.

Yet the irony is that his own real needs were not really met. Created in the image of God, he never managed to grasp his own identity or its ramifications. He never probed beyond the gifts to the One who freely and graciously bestowed them on him. Being unable to respond to the needs of those around him, he never encountered the Divine in the face of another.

Recall St. Paul writing to the church in Corinth asking for money for the church in Jerusalem. Paul and the church leaders in Jerusalem had serious disagreements and had maintained an uneasy fellowship, yet Paul's understanding of Christian philanthropy was unassailable. The people needed to support each other whether they agreed or not. They were to give not reluctantly or compulsively, but willingly, because God loves a cheerful giver, one who gives as an expression of thanks to God for his indescribable gift to us.

I remember sitting in an office at the Chapel of the Cross filling in for the rector, who was away. A member of the parish who had been vocally critical of the '79 prayer book entered and said, "I want to talk about the prayer book." I thought, "Why isn't the rector here? I'm just a non-stipendiary priest; he gets paid to listen to complaints." Then, I'll always remember, he said, "I just learned that two of my friends didn't pledge this year. I asked them what they gave last year. Here's a check for their pledge and mine. I'll never like the damn book, but this is family, so you don't vote with your wallet, and anyway, God has been so good to me, what real choice do I have unless I'm going to be ungrateful."

Holding up the people's offering of bread and wine, I sometimes say, "God, you gave us this bread and wine to offer. Gifts of creation and the work of our human hands, they will become for us our spiritual food and drink." In our worship we give thanks for all the gifts of life undeservedly received. We therefore bring our gifts—our offering—as our response. God accepts our gifts and gives them back to us as nourishment for life in God's reign where the care and stewardship of life are life's goal. True worship, then, is an alternating rhythm of consumption and contribution, the receiving of gifts and the giving of alms.

Von Christierson, who began his great stewardship hymn "As those of old their first fruits brought . . ." (705, Hymnal 1982), ends it with these words: "With gratitude and humble trust we bring our best to thee, to serve thy cause and share thy love with all humanity. O thou who gavest us thyself in Jesus Christ thy Son, help us to give ourselves each day until life's work is done."

Mixed Views on Faith and Money

Robert Wuthnow, director of the Center for the Study of American Religion at Princeton University, has for years studied our views on faith and money and discovered that the subject of money evokes deep ambivalence within most of us. On the one hand the sentiment prevails that our culture emphasizes money and material goods too much. On the other hand most people are terribly interested in money, and few seem able to decide when enough is enough.

Most acknowledge that materialism is a serious problem in our society. They sense that our wants are spiraling out of control. They know that there is more to life than nice things, and they are dimly aware of biblical teaching contrasting the worship of God and mammon. Yet few are convinced that there might be a conflict between valuing our relationship with God and valuing making a lot of money. Most are able to rationalize their way out of positions the Scriptures take on money. What most of us appear to do is to take the Christian faith and add a dollop of piety to the materialistic amalgam in which we desire to live. We do not feel compelled to give up any of our material desires, only to put them in a self-chosen perspective.

Believing that materialism is a serious problem, however, seems to have little to do with how we live. Money and material possessions are, in fact, among the things we cherish most deeply, and we readily admit our attachment to things. Money is regarded as providing us with greater freedom, and having it gives us a good feeling about ourselves. Few believe that wealthy people are happier than others, but most of us harbor the conviction that having just a little more money would make us happier.

17

While most people think that God does care about how we use our money, faith appears to have little to do with the ways we actually conduct our financial affairs. Money is considered too personal to be talked about openly. The darkest taboo in our country is not sex or death but our personal finances. For many, money is considered to be value free. Therefore, faith, morals and values have little to do with money. Perhaps this explains why clergy typically avoid the issue. Stewardship, it appears, is understood at best as charitable giving and a very private matter about which we would prefer not to speak or hear sermons.

Necessary Subversion

Now remember, parables are intended to subvert how we see things so that we might see through the eyes of God, that is, receive the gift of faith. In a wonderful parable that is often misinterpreted, Jesus tells us of a dishonest manager (Luke 16:1–13).

There was a rich man who had a steward, and charges were brought against him claiming that he was keeping more than his rightful fee for services and sending less than he should to the owner who employed him. So the rich owner wrote him and said, "What is this I hear about you. Turn in an account of your stewardship." The steward pondered what he would do: "I am not in good enough shape to work as a peasant and I am ashamed to beg, so I know what I'll do—I'll contact each one of the peasants and ask what they owe, and I will eliminate the extra amount I had added so that they will be beholden to me and my employer will still receive his full due." It was a prudent act, and the wealthy businessman praised him for cleverly ensuring his future security. And Jesus comments, "It appears that the children of this world can be wiser than the children of light." What is this parable about? Why was the wicked steward commended?

Jesus explains it this way. If only Christians were as eager and ingenious in their desire to attain a right relationship with God as this dishonest steward was to build a relationship with the peasants who worked for him so that he could get their pity and help, we would be more happy, that is, blessed. If only we all would give as much attention to the things that concern our souls as we do to the things that concern our business, the world would be in better shape. If only we would expend as much time and effort on our spiritual life as we do on the attainment of money, material comfort and personal pleasure, the reign of God might come into its fullness.

We need to get our priorities straight and be faithful to what has been entrusted to us. We are to make sure that wealth and material possessions always remain a means of serving God and never become ends in themselves.

As Jesus reminds us, we cannot serve God and wealth. And as Martin Luther knew, we humans need to experience three conversions: of heart, mind and purse. Perhaps this explains why Jesus spoke about money more than any other issue. He knew that it is the key to our spiritual life and that money can be used either to enhance or threaten our relationship with God.

19

In spite of the radio evangelists who try to convince us that if we love Jesus we will get rich, it just doesn't work that way. Neither is poverty a sign of God's displeasure. Jesus taught a spirituality of poverty but did not advocate penury. Penury is having nothing, which would imply that since the poor are blessed we would have no good reason to address their needs. The virtue of poverty, on the other hand, means not being attached to what we have so that we can give freely and generously to those in need. So it is that the root sin of avarice is the love of possessing.

Money and how we think of it is never neutral. Have you heard a child ask for something and the parents reply, "We cannot afford it"? That, of course, implies that if they could afford it they would buy it. Perhaps a better response might be, "Let us pray about it and see if God thinks we need it." And when we look about and see all we have, why not ask God to reveal to us how better we might use or share what we have as ministry, that is, our way to serve God and fulfill our vocation to grow into an ever deepening and loving relationship with God.

Regretfully, the modern hero we present to children is someone who came from a simple, humble, poor beginning and rose to the heights of wealth and position, not the humble Francis or Clare who gave up wealth and status to become poor and live lives of simplicity. In our society we sometimes label covetousness ambition, hoarding prudence, greed industry pride, achievement avarice success.

In that regard I read a strange story in a newspaper a few years ago. It was about a wealthy man who had retired and then volunteered to be the sexton in his parish church. One day, it seems, he was kneeling in front of a statue as he was cleaning the floor and he heard a voice: "Go sell what you have and give it to the poor and follow me." It was so

powerful and real that he withdrew his money from the bank and gave it
to the church. After he stuffed it in the poor box, he started walking up
the road that he had heard led to a monastery. When his neighbors
discovered he had not returned, they reported him missing. The police
eventually found him and placed him in a mental hospital for observa-
tion. In time a psychiatrist acknowledged that the man was not insane
but needed to be in a nursing home where he could be watched over.
Once upon a time another man kneeling before the same statue heard
the same voice. His name was Francis. Francis was made a saint, yet
this man in our day almost labeled mad.

We Are an Endowed People

Once a parishioner asked me, "Why is the church so interested in
money? It seems like that's all we think and talk about." While that
just isn't true, I chose not to argue but instead answered, "I suspect it is
because that is what people are most interested in." Isn't the nation's
most widely circulated newspaper, after all, the *Wall Street Journal*,
which is almost entirely given to the subject of money and matters that
pertain to producing and holding wealth? And isn't one of the most
popular PBS programs *Wall Street Week*?

"So what has that to do with church?" he pressed. And I replied, "As
Anglicans we have always taken seriously the theological doctrine of the

incarnation, namely that God chose to enter into our humanity and live in our social world, thereby forever uniting the material and the non-material, the sacred and the secular, the natural and the supernatural. For this reason the Christian faith will always be materialistic. The test of our relationship with God will always be seen in how we deal with our economic resources. The spiritual challenge is to make our money work for what is really important in God's eyes. There is a dark side to money in that it can be a threat to our relationship with God. And there is a light side to money in that it can enhance our relationship with God." He replied, "That's an interesting twist. I'll have to think about it."

Soon thereafter I left that parish, and so I may never know whether my remarks had any effect. Since then, however, I have reflected on that conversation many times. In the process I have discovered that our English word "money" has its roots in the early Latin word *moneo*, which means "to recollect." Among the numerous thoughts we need to recollect is that we are an endowed people, endowed by God and endowed by the wealth of the past bestowed upon us by our ancestors.

The endowment, the inheritance, out of which we all live was made possible mostly by God and a nameless host of people who went before us. Some knew poverty and others wealth, but all left us a goodly heritage. And I suspect this was done with the expectation that we in gratitude would do the same for others we ourselves will never know.

Each and every one of us has been endowed by God and those who went before us. Our lives are "gifted" from beginning to end, and it is inconceivable that it could be otherwise. So it is that the future of generations yet to come depends on our willingness to leave behind an endowment upon which they can build for the work of Christ and his church.

The wealth we each create through the expenditures of our time and energy does not and must not accrue for us alone. We need to acknowledge that we live on an endowment bestowed upon us and that the same needs to be a portion of the legacy we leave at the time of our death. It is our way of expressing gratitude to those who have empowered our lives.

As you might expect, I am an advocate of planned giving, but I become somewhat troubled when I hear some of the reasons offered for leaving part of our inheritance to the church, namely that it will benefit us now and our families in the future. As Christians we are judged for our motives as well as our actions. We must do the right thing, but the right thing for the right reason. To defend endowments solely by pointing out how everyone benefits is questionably a faithful reason. We need to support the building of endowments whether we benefit or not. Our rationale needs to be based on gratitude to God and those who have endowed us in ages past.

Let us never forget that most of us each Sunday gather in a house of worship others built. We listen to an organ and gaze upon stained-glass windows; we take wine and bread from patens and chalices left to us by others. If our parish has an endowment we may enjoy air-conditioning repaired by gifts of those who never experienced air-conditioning. We may be able to care for the needy in ways we never could have without others' having left us the resources for doing so. Most congregations could be more faithful to the demands of the moment if those who went before them had had an understanding of stewardship that went beyond the present and had willingly made a commitment to a future they would never enjoy, whether or not they benefited from the gift.

Churches and dioceses with endowments are churches and dioceses in which other generations took seriously a faithful understanding of

23

stewardship. Each generation needs to invest in those things that matter most to God, not because they will benefit by doing so but because it is the faithful thing to do. In one important sense the church does not need our money as much as we need to give it to the church. It is important for each of us to give from what we have acquired in our lifetime not only to the ministry of the church in our day but to the ministry of the church after we have gone. By giving toward the churches' endowments we can be in community with those who will come after us. We demonstrate our trust that God will be present and active in the church after we are gone, inspiring another generation to live faithfully. It is the gifts of our ancestors—the communion of saints—that unite us with them in ministry, and it will be our gifts that will unite us with those to be baptized into that communion in generations to come.

The theological issue, however, is greater than giving in gratitude for the gifts of others. Remember that all things—including the economic resources given by our forebears as well as those resources we may believe and the law says we own—belong to God. Both our endowments and our own resources are entrusted to us only for use in the service of God's will. We therefore need grateful and generous hearts and the will to give of our lives and resources. Not to give generously with a grateful heart is to choose stagnation, like the Dead Sea, which has no outlet for what the Jordan River feeds it. To let ourselves, on the other hand, be a conduit for God's gifts is to choose life, like the Sea of Galilee, fed by the same Jordan River, which both receives and gives.

What we have has been entrusted to us for a purpose, namely so that we might do something faithful with it and thus through our stewardship grow in our spiritual life and through our spiritual life become more faithful stewards. One of the primary ways we are to use what we have been given is to give it away, particularly for faithful causes from which we will never benefit directly. We give because to do otherwise is to stifle the life-giving flow of gifts over time and to choose stagnation and the eventual death of all from which we have benefited.

Good Stewards of God's Grace

The Scriptures do not support the individualism characterized by our culture; rather, they understand human nature as communal and inter-dependent. The Scriptures, therefore, take exception to the popular notion of the absolute right of private property. The earth belongs only to God and therefore cannot be held by anyone as if it were his or her possession. That is why in the year of the jubilee (one in every fifty years) all land was to revert back to its original owner (Leviticus, Chapter 25). In fact, the purpose of the year of the jubilee was to pro-vide a regular redistribution of wealth so that the poor would not get poorer and the rich richer. Why? Because all wealth was viewed as belonging to God and therefore to all equally.

The Scriptures affirm the material world but have no sympathy with materialism, that is, with a preoccupation with material reality which either denies or ignores nonmaterial reality. Hedonism (a preoccupation with pleasure or material happiness as the chief goal of life) and narcissism (a preoccupation with the love of oneself, especially one's physical attributes) are both severely judged. For the Scriptures our love is to be directed to God, the chief goal of life being doing God's will.

While most of us have been socialized to live acquisitively, Jesus proposed a different motivation for life's activities. His words were, "Be on your guard against all kinds of greed" (Luke 12:15) and "Whoever would be great among you must be your servant" (Mark 10:43). It is not in serving oneself but in losing one's life in the service of another's good that we find our true selves. "Let no one seek his own good, but the good of his neighbor" (2 Corinthians 10:24).

The Scriptures forbid any sense of human ownership of anything in creation. In Genesis God creates man and woman to tend, care for, and share with others all of creation. The earth and its resources have been given to us in trust so that we might use them to sustain the whole human family. God intends us to be trustees of the possessions, property, and productive capital placed in our keeping by seeking to use them for God's purposes, that is, for the good of all humanity. Stewardship does not imply the complete renunciation of ownership of material possession, but it does imply the acknowledgment that we are held accountable for how these possessions are acquired and how they are used.

That explains why in Christian ethics almsgiving has always been treated under the heading of justice rather than mercy. Giving to meet a neighbor's need is in actuality only giving to others what is rightfully theirs.

26

Therefore, our contributions to individuals in need, to community social service agencies and voluntary associations, and to the church mission and ministry are simply obligatory acts of stewardship for which we deserve no thanks or reward. Thus we are not to think of our charity as an act of mercy for the less fortunate. We are only given the freedom to be responsible or irresponsible stewards of God's wealth. The implications are vast. In short, stewardship is concerned with nothing less than our responsibility for every aspect of individual and social life within every aspect of life. Stewardship is the active recognition of the sovereignty of God over all creation, over all the creative and productive processes in which we human share, and over the uses to which we put each and every resource and means that comes into our care and control.

Stewardship Is More Than Money

Remember our earlier contention that a yearly pledge of time, talent, and money, based upon programmatic budgetary needs to run an institution and its laudatory programs, is not an acceptable understanding of stewardship. Nevertheless, as stewards of God we are invited to join in God's actions, God's mission in the world. We are, remember,

Christ's body, God's sacrament, so that Christ can be present through us in human life and history. It is for this sacramental purpose that God calls us into the church.

We are to live our lives in the interest of fulfilling God's will. And the more we have been given, the more will be expected of us. We need not, for example, feel guilty for having abundant food, so long as the energy and joy we receive from it are devoted to the needs and happiness of the hungry. "Bless this food to our use and us to your service, while keeping us ever mindful of the needs of others," we pray.

All that we are and have—our lives, intelligence, imagination, sensibilities, abilities, potential for growth and inheritance—are gifts from God, given to us to be developed and used for the benefit of all God's children. Stewardship begins with a recognition that God is a generous giver and that we are called upon to be a grateful, responsive, and responsible people. In the words of St. Peter (1 Peter 4:10–11), "Like good stewards of the manifold grace of God, serve one another with whatever gift each of you has received. . . . Whoever serves must do so with the strength that God supplies, so that God may be glorified in all things through Jesus Christ. To him belong the glory and the power forever and ever. Amen."

In writing this monograph I was saddened to discover how little attention is given to stewardship in books on liturgics, ethics, spirituality, pastoral care, Christian education, or the church's mission and ministry. It was for that reason I wrote in 1983 *Building God's People in a Materialistic Society*. While it was a book on stewardship that dealt with each of these dimensions of practical theology, it was not a popular book. It was also generally missing on reading lists published by denominational stewardship offices. The only explanation I can arrive at is that stewardship was not a popular subject and those who were entrusted with stewardship conceived of it primarily in terms of raising money and building endowments for the institutional church rather than as a theological and moral issue that relates to every aspect of our personal and communal lives.

Still at the Heart of Stewardship Is Money

I had a colleague at Duke who regularly either shocked or angered people by saying that he was not interested in their faith biographies but that he would like to hear the story of their life and money. Or he would comment following a conversation on the stewardship of time and talents, or the stewardship of nature, "Please share with me your checkbook, your credit card records and your tax forms for the past five years. Then I'll really understand your faith and your understanding of stewardship." Behind those questions, of course, lies the biblical wisdom that "where your treasure is, there is your heart also" (Matthew 6:21).

Nevertheless, it is difficult to get most people to talk honestly about their money. One day I was having lunch at the Duke faculty club with a visiting professor from Korea. At one point he commented, "In the

United States people in the course of casual conversation will tell you the details of a recent surgical operation or intimate family problems but never tell you anything about their economic life. I also have discovered that it is rude and inappropriate to ask."

It is as if we think money is evil and not to be discussed. But money is not evil—it is the love of money that is the root of evil. That is, money is a temptation. It urges us to put our confidence in it rather than in God. We humans seem to prefer to trust what we can see and touch and control to what we cannot control, but God promises and gives to those who put their trust in and dependence upon him.

It is interesting to note that the Hebrew word for money, kesef, comes from the verb "to desire or languish after," which stresses the spiritual character of money as well as its power. It also points to the fact that regardless of how much money we acquire, we will never be satisfied; we will always desire more, believing that we will be happier if we do. So it is that advertizing encourages us to buy, to possess and to accumulate more and more, and, worse, even convince us that in so doing we ourselves actually become more. Only over time do we come to realize that we do not own our possessions, that they own us, and by then we have lost our souls.

Recall the rich man who came in search of life with God (Luke 18:18–22). Jesus invites him to follow in a way that is centered on God: "Sell what you own and give the money to God." To say yes would have meant to let go of wealth, possession, and his self-image of a good and faithful person. To say yes to a new and untried way of life, one totally dependent upon God and one in which he would get no credit or thanks for his beneficence, was more than he could imagine or desire. And so like many of us he was unable.

Over the years I have struggled with stewardship and painfully have come to the conclusion that stewardship is not just generous gifts to good causes but an attitude toward life. For example, there are those who from their wealth pledge to the work of the church but are more apt to give significant amounts to special causes. They will write on request a personal check for repairs, a new organ, a stained-glass window, vestments or some other need of the church they approve of and want to support. It appears as if they like to be asked, to make a personal decision of the value of the request, and perhaps receive some recognition, publicly or privately in terms of influence, for their generosity. The church does benefit and the giver deserves the church's gratitude, but my concern is spiritual. What do such forms of generosity say about our understanding and vision of stewardship? What do they have to do with our relationship with God and the salvation of our souls?

A Stewardship Vision

In Genesis, in the beginning, humanity is given food by God. Food is a gift of God. We are to take it and share it, not hoard, possess or overindulge in it. Having fed us, Jesus calls us to feed others. "Feed my sheep," he says (John 21:15–17).

For too long we have been concerned with what happens to the bread and wine at Eucharist. The real issue is what happens to those who consume it. We who come to Eucharist need to be aware that we are what we eat and then ponder what it implies that we take the life of Christ into our bodies. That is how the Eucharist judges our consumer society and its values, a society in which some eat and eat and are never satisfied while others go hungry.

In Deuteronomy we read, "If there is among you anyone in need . . . in the land the Lord has given you, do not be hard-hearted or tight-fisted toward your needy neighbor. You should open your hand, willingly lending enough to meet the need. . . . Be careful not to entertain a mean thought, thinking, 'the seventh year, the year of debt remission is near' and therefore view your needy neighbor with hostility and give nothing. . . . Give liberally and be ungrudging when you do so, for on this account the Lord your God will bless you in all you undertake. Since there will never cease to be some in need on earth, I therefore command you 'Open your hand to the poor and the needy neighbor in your land' " (Deuteronomy 15:7–11).

Or consider the words of Paul to the church in Corinth: "I am testing the genuineness of your love, for you know the generous act of our Lord Jesus Christ, that though he was rich yet for our sakes he became poor, so that by his poverty you might become rich. I do not mean that there should be relief for others and pressure on you, but it is a question of a just balance between your present abundance and their need. . . . As it is written, 'The one who had much did not have too much and the one who had little did not have too little.' " (2 Corinthians 8:1–9, 13–15).

The Scriptures contain a vision of society in which the wealth of one person cannot be based upon the exploitation of another and in which the conviction that we are all members of a single human family leads those with abundance to supply the wants of all others until the goal of equality is reached (2 Corinthians 8:14). The Scriptures picture a God who wants us to live as stewards of every aspect of human life and the natural world. All our material resources, time, energy and talents are to be devoted to joining God in making possible a world of *shalom*, a world not only of peace but of well-being, health, harmony, equity, unity, freedom, and community.

The central vision in the Scriptures for life in this world is one in which all creation is one, every creature in community with every other creature, living in harmony and security toward the joy and well-being of every other creature. Therefore, stewardship is concerned with our growing into an ever deepening and loving relationship with our true self, the self in the image of God, with all people, and with the natural world. But we need to acknowledge that this end is dependent upon our growing into an ever deepening and loving relationship with God. Love God and then love neighbor and self equally. The spiritual comes before the material.

The Spirituality of Stewardship

Stewardship is about giving up the love of possessing and practicing a life of simplicity: of developing the habit of giving things away; of buying only what is absolutely necessary; of rejecting anything to which we are becoming addicted; of learning to enjoy things without owning them; of developing a greater appreciation of and respect for the natural world; of rejecting anything that will result in an injustice for others.

This life of simplicity, however, is first an inward reality, an inward reality that results in an outward lifestyle. While we cannot have one without the other, simplicity, like every other aspect of the spiritual life, begins with an inward journey.

If we are ever to nurture ourselves and others to understand and be good stewards, we need to begin with the spiritual life. No courses or books, no sermons or inspirational lectures, will achieve our goal, which is to nurture persons and communities who deal with wealth, material possessions, with time and the use of talents in ways that are a sign and witness to God's reign, that condition in which God's will is known and done.

Only if we nourish and nurture the spiritual life—that is, learn to live in an ever deepening and loving relationship with God—will we ever be able to be aware of and acknowledge that all that we have is a gift from God, a consequence of God's grace, God's loving presence and action in our lives. We need to be aware of and acknowledge that we live by grace and are dependent upon God for the simplest elements of life. And so it is that we do not need so much and can generously share what we have with others. For too long we have made the error of talking about limited resources. We forget that as soon as people believe there may not be enough, they begin to hoard rather than share. But when we are confident that God will see that our deepest, most basic needs are met, we can live in trust and with hope, sharing what we have with all who are in need.

To illustrate how the attitudes which result from a healthy spiritual life lead to actions that demonstrate a healthy, grateful heart, I would like to tell a story of Charles Lamb, among the most lovable and charming characters in English literary history. Lamb lived a tragic life. His mentally ill sister murdered his mother. He had to take care of his sick, demanding, critical father, and he worked long hours for little pay. Once he wrote to his friend Coleridge: "I am starving at the India House. It is near eight p.m. and I have had nothing to eat this day. It has been the same for months. Still, when I arrive home weary and faint my father insists I play cards with him. I pray for the most part I am not ungrateful." Charles Lamb had a grateful and generous heart. But it was not the result of a happy, prosperous life. It was the result of his faith and his relationship with God.

Further, to illustrate how the convictions which result from a healthy spiritual life lead to acts that demonstrate a generous heart, I would like to share a story I was told while teaching in Japan a number of years ago. A peasant who was a Christian lived on a high hill. One day he saw a tidal wave approaching on the tail of an earthquake. His neighbors in the valley were ignorant of the danger. He set fire to his fields and rang the church bell. They hurried up the hill to help him. When they saw that he was burning the fields they were furious, yet, turning back, they saw that the tidal wave had destroyed their village. They asked him why he did what he did, and he told them about Christ's sacrificial love and how in gratitude he was sharing that with them.

Stewardship is not a program or campaign, and it is not about raising money for the church budget—it is a way of life, a way of life that issues forth naturally from Christian faith and spiritual life. Once we have all grown in our relationship with God and therefore in faith, hope, and love, we will never again have to worry about church finances or have a stewardship campaign. Then the economics of God will make sense and stewardship will become a natural dimension of our Christian life of faith.

"God of grace and God of glory," Harry Emerson Fosdick's well-known hymn written during the Great Depression petitions, ". . . shame our wanton, selfish gladness, rich in things and poor in soul. Grant us wisdom, grant us courage, lest we miss thy kingdom's goal" (595, Hymnal 1982).

Fosdick could not have imagined the richness in things that we know today. Our unprecedented wealth and prosperity, unchecked and ill managed, have led us to a poverty of the soul and a new quest for the spiritual life. We seem to have realized that we have become the incarnate answer to the eternal truth, "For what does it profit us to gain the whole world and lose our own souls?" (Matthew 16:26).

The well-known and loved nun Mother Teresa was born into a wealthy, prestigious family. At thirty-eight while on retreat she received a call similar to St. Francis' to abandon everything she had grown up to love and enjoy and go to work with the poorest of the poor in Calcutta, India.

I taught one summer in a seminary in Bangladesh and she paid us a visit. Among the comments she made at lunch to these middle-class seminarians was the following: "I hope you are not giving to the church and its mission to the poor only of your abundance. You must give what costs you dearly. Make a sacrifice of something you need and desire so that your gift may be of value before God. And then you will become brothers and sisters to the poor who are deprived of what they need and desire." Reflecting on that experience, I concluded that both poverty and affluence are the failure of faithful stewardship and the consequence of an atrophied spiritual life.

Last Thoughts

Alan Jones provides us with an illuminating commentary on Graham Greene's novel *Dr. Fischer of Geneva or the Bomb Party*. As Jones writes, "the heroes of Greene's novels are often struggling in search of their own souls, or to put it in our words, to develop their spiritual lives."[2] In this particular novel, Greene describes the four requirements necessary for human beings to live in an ever deepening and loving relationship with God.[3]

At one point, Greene's hero is talking with his wife about her malicious father, Dr. Fischer, and his strange friends. She asks, "Have you a soul?"

"I think I have one—shop-worn but still there, but if souls exist you certainly have one."

"Why?"

"You've suffered."

One of Dr. Fischer's friends is Monsieur Belmont, a busy lawyer who specializes in tax evasion. As for a soul, "he hasn't time to develop one. . . . A soul requires a private life. Belmont has no time for a private life."

There is also a soldier, the Divisionnaire, who "might possibly have a soul. There's something unhappy about him."

"And Mr. Kips?"

"I'm not sure about him either. There's a sense of disappointment about him. He might be looking for something he mislaid. Perhaps he's looking for his soul and not a dollar."

Then there is Richard Deane, the aging movie idol. "No, definitely not. No soul. I'm told he has copies of his old films and he plays them over every night to himself. . . . He's satisfied with himself. If you have a soul you can't be satisfied."

There we have Graham Greene's four requirements for living a spiritual life: a willingness to embrace suffering, our own and the world's; a life marked by moments of silence and solitude; a willingness to pay attention to the deep restlessness in our spirit; and life within a community of faith that sees the image of God, the image of Christ, in us.

If we are to live in an ever deepening and loving relationship with God, we need to live out of the depths of life, identifying with all who suffer. This sense of compassion underlies grateful and generous hearts. If we are to be aware of the presence and action of God in our lives and history, we need to be alone and silent. This consciousness of God nurtures grateful and generous hearts. And if we are, with God's help, to know and do God's will, we need to pay attention to the deep restlessness in our interior lives. This ability will lead us to have grateful and generous hearts.

Let us recall that the commandment is to love God fully first and then, secondly, as the natural consequence, to love self and neighbor equally as God loves us. Nourish and nurture the spiritual life first and the moral life will follow. Nourish and nurture good stewards by beginning with a spiritual-life emphasis. Put aside traditional stewardship education programs and begin to worship and pray together. Stewardship and the economics of God, like faith, cannot be taught, but they can be caught, nurtured and lived into. And that is the ever present challenge before us, a challenge that with God's help is forever possible.

Scripture quotations are taken from the *New Revised Standard Version* of the Bible. Copyright ©1989 by the Division of Christian Education of the National Council of the Churches of Christ in the United States.

[1]Oursler, Fulton. *Behold This Dreamer.* Boston: Little, Brown, 1964.

[2]Jones, Alan. *Exploring Spiritual Direction.* New York: Seabury Press, 1982. 23–25.

[3]Greene, Graham. *Dr. Fischer of Geneva, or the Bomb Party.* New York: Simon & Schuster, 1980. 192–194.

The Rev. Dr. John Westerhoff is an Episcopal priest on the staff of St. Luke's Episcopal Church in Atlanta, Georgia, and director of the Institute for Pastoral Studies, the publisher of this monograph. For twenty years he was Professor of Theology and Christian Nurture at the Duke University Divinity School. He has written over thirty books, including the classic *Will Our Children Have Faith?* He is married to Caroline, Canon for Congregational Life and Ministry in the Diocese of Atlanta and author of *Calling: A Song for the Baptized.*

CPSIA information can be obtained
at www.ICGtesting.com
Printed in the USA
LVOW05s1410100217
523686LV00001B/1/P